...let there be light

ISBN: 978-81-7436-600-9

M-75 Greater Kailash-II (Market)
New Delhi 110 048, India.
Phone: +91-11-2921 2271, 2921 2782
Fax: +91-11-2921 7185
Email: roli@vsnl.com Website: rolibooks.com

Design:	Parthiv Shah
Design assistance:	Shraboni Roy, CMAC
Text edit:	Sonal Parmar
Production:	Kumar Raman

Special thanks:	Prof. Kapil Kapoor (RgVeda translations)
	Sanjeev Saith (Picture selection)

Printed and bound in Singapore

"You are *jyoti-svarupa*"; your self-form is the illumining form of light. You have been established for mankind and for the sake of his other directed activities you become *prakasamana*, effulgent.

Invocation addressed to *Agni*
Rgveda hymn 1.36.19b

...let there be light

exploring nature through light

photographs by mahesh nair

edited by dr. alka pande

Lustre Press
Roli Books

Sarawak, Borneo

contents

Pangong Tso, Ladakh

making the invisible visible

dr. alka pande

Light makes photography. Embrace light. Admire it. Love it. But above all, know light. Know it for all you are worth, and you will know the key to photography.

- George Eastman

Mahesh's love for photography and his engagement with light cannot be contested. This corporate honcho finally took the plunge in 2005 to follow his first love, photography, and remain true to the medium.

An engineer by training, for Mahesh the meticulous eye for detail, precision for the technical, and a knowledge of the mechanical aspects of photography were a given. What intrigued, inspired and invoked Mahesh was one of the key elements of photography itself - light. For him, the immediacy of the medium became the "guru" mantra. For the last five years he has been exploring, enriching and fine-tuning his own personal vocabulary with light remaining a constant in his language.

In many ways Mahesh is a traditionalist, and is pursuing photography in its purest form. His pictures are representative of all the elements of what makes a good photograph. His work is almost canonical, his genre removed from the more recent popular styles of image-making, which traverse the domain of documentary, photo journalism, fine art, conceptual and experimental genres.

When I first saw Mahesh's pictures some years ago, I was intrigued by the manner in which he captured the essence of light in his own image-making. In a way "light" becomes a recurring leitmotif in his work; whether he is looking at flora or fauna or simply capturing a moment, light seems to be his constant muse.

With light Mahesh centres himself. He chases it, seduces it, captures it, and even challenges it. And it is his feverish obsession with the phenomenon that he reminds me of a similar engagement with light which engaged the Dutch masters right through to the French Impressionists.

It was Tony Palazzo, artist and film maker, who stated that the Dutch genre painters, especially Jan Steen, were the first documentary artists. Through the art-historical narrative against which I wish to read, contextualize and explore Mahesh's work, it is clear that photography was seen in European painting when romanticism was widely admired and was also commercially successful. Whether it was the highly sensual and romantic Eugene Delacroix, whose work was embedded in turbulent fiction and exotic allegories, or the brash young French painter Gustave Courbet, photography was generously welcomed into the fold. Both of them and many others like Edgar Degas, Edvard Munch, and Ernst Kirchner

all started using photography to improve their own art form. With time they all became accomplished photographers.

An example of a picture with "painterly light" would be Louis Daguerre's *Boulevard du Temple* (1838) which happened to be the first photograph of a person. Delacroix went a notch further. He wrote in his diary that "if a man of genius should use the daguerreotype as it ought to be used, he will raise himself to heights unknown to us." A number of painters even used photographs to reference details like facial expression, and ephemeral light effect. In fact, a visual reading of some of my favourite European painters reveals that even they painted from photographic sketches, something which we as art-historians sometimes tend to forget.

Pierre Bonnard (1867-1947) showed particular skill and sensitivity in suggesting a sense of light and colour flickering on the canvas as if it were a tapestry. His compositions were typically of sunlit rooms and gardens populated with friends and family members, and both were narrative and autobiographical in tone. Bonnard's painting titled *At the Table* (1899) is an apt example of painterly light in his works.

Paul Gauguin lent a mysterious and ethereal effect to his paintings. A vase of flowers is one of his works well known for its painterly qualities. As the French poet Mallarme put it so aptly, "Gauguin put so much mystery into so much brightness."

Renoir is well known for the use of vibrant light in his works. Through the practice of painting light and water en plein air, in the late 1860s, along with Claude Monet he discovered that the colour of shadows is not brown or black, but the reflected colour of the objects surrounding them.

Rembrandt is well known for his use of chiaroscuro, the theatrical employment of light and shadow derived from the 16th century painter Caravaggio. Photographers have for a long time tried to emulate "Rembrandt Lighting" in their works. In studio portraiture, one side of the face is well lit and the other side has a combination of shadow and light.

Caravaggio, in fact, is one of the painters in whose work light plays a dramatic role. They are characteristics of his paintings. Until this point in time paintings were carried out by drawings and colours, but Caravaggio introduced a third element, light. It can enter through a window out of the frame or through a vision from the sky; it lightens faces, hands, bodies, is reflected on draperies and creates dark shadow areas wherever it doesn't arrive. The scene becomes united and compact because of this contrast which is sometimes even violent.

Although Caravaggio's short and troubled life didn't allow him access to anyone to whom he could transmit his knowledge and success, the radical novelty of the times inaugurated a school and a taste which won him followers from across Italy and Europe. In fact, Caravaggio's use of light still has an indelible influence on modern cinema.

According to Martin Scorese, "If Caravaggio were alive today, he would have loved the cinema; his paintings take a cinematic approach. We film-makers became aware of his work in the late 1960s and early 1970s, and he certainly was an influence on us."

Ever since the introduction of photography in 1837, there has been an incestuous relationship between painting and photography. In the present post-structuralist world with the blurring of boundaries between art practices and theory, an entire new language of conceptual art has been added to the fine-art realm. The compartmentalized genres of art and materials were brushed under the carpet when conceptual art came of age. Artists like Gerhard Richter, David Hockney, and Moni K. Huber, Joel-Peter Witkin, and Eddy de Vos started looking at and using photographs and painting in a symbiotic manner. To explicate further, Gerhard Richter started creating paintings by altering photographs.

Photography took a dramatic turn in the second part of the 20th century when Steiglitz started using his own New York Gallery to promote a modern style of photography, as in the works of Paul Strand *(The White Fence)*. Steiglitz became the catalyst who turned photography into an art medium. In fact, he used the same sharp focus in portraits of his wife, the painter Georgia O'Keefe. Within modernism, the American Paul Strand, the Hungarian born Bauhaus protagonist Laszlo Moholgy-Nagy, used photography as a tool of cultural representation. Maholgy–Nagy categorically stated that the camera held the key to the "New Vision". He went beyond the camera and produced photograms and photomontages. Artists like Aleksandr Rodchenko who were involved with Russian constructivism shared the belief of the power of photography. Edward Weston and John Szarowski took the exploration of personal expression through photography even further.

A parallel relationship between photography and painting is keenly contested by photographers who greeted amateur photography or snapshots taken by the masses or "Kodakers" with dismay. Alfred Stieglitz, Holland Day and Gertrude Kasebier were key figures for the "pictorialists", and used specialized and complex darkroom techniques to foreground their own singular technique.

In his classic essay, Clive Bell states that only "significant form" can distinguish art from what is not art.

"There must be some one quality without which a work of art cannot exist; possessing which, in the least degree, no work is altogether worthless. What is this quality? What quality is shared by all objects that provoke our aesthetic emotions? What quality is common to Sta. Sophia and the windows at Chartres, Mexican sculpture, a Persian bowl, Chinese carpets, Giotto's frescoes at Padua, and the masterpieces of Poussin, Piero della Francesca, and Cezanne? Only one answer seems possible - significant form. In each, lines and colours combined in a particular way, certain forms and relations of forms, stir our aesthetic emotions."

When photography entered the hallowed portals of "art" somewhere in the early 1890s, painters reacted strongly to it. In a way its invention led to the liberation of realism in painting. A lot of modern painting in the 20th century could be read as a reaction to his trend. It is said that Kandinsky painted his first abstract painting in 1911, more than half a century after the introduction of photography.

"It takes a lot of imagination to be a good photographer. You need less imagination to be a painter, because you can invent things. But in photography everything is so ordinary; it takes a lot of looking before you learn to see the ordinary."
David Bailey

Photography in its initial stages often served as a handmaiden to painting. Within the Indian context, the first archival records in reading photography come in the way of the vast resources left to us by way of colonial photography. The "Alkazi Collection" consisting of 40,000 pictures becomes the largest single source, a delight for any scholar on Indian photography. Whether they are Beato's albums, Bourne and Shepherd's, or Lala Deen Dayal's photographic studios, photography was primarily used as documentation for architects, politicians or the social documentation of events. A photograph never lied, and it was in the reading of it that it became a cultural tool, an anthropologists delight, and a newspaper record. With time it evolved to become the best possible archival record.

Photography critic, writer and lecturer from North America, Vicki Goldberg, put it succinctly. " Victoria was fascinated by the jewel in her crown, and so were her subjects. She hired Indian servants, one of whom became quite influential." Photographs show the Queen at table with Indian menservants standing by, looking suitably foreign and imposing; pictures of the Queen being served by representatives of her largest colony must have been a matter of some pride to the populace. She also sent British artists abroad to paint the newest members of her realm.

But photography was the great recorder of the age and the medium of choice in a land that not only entranced and enriched the British but also bewildered them by never being quite what it seemed. Britons, other foreigners and large numbers of Indians all hastened to register India's astonishing variety and explore the countries at its borders.

A similar point is made by Sunil Khilnani, according to whom, the photographs in *India through the Lens* and *India: Pioneering Photographers*, testify handsomely to the technical and aesthetic quality of the work that resulted from the Indian embrace of photography. John Falconer in his book, *Pioneering Indian Photographers*, gives a sensitive overview of the development of photography, and Vidya Dehejia too looks at the similar frame with her own language.

There can be no denying that colonial Indian photography has had its precious moments and will continue to do so. But what is of immediate concern to me right now is the burst of photographic practices and the burgeoning of

photographers in India. in India. In a country where photography is not really being "taught", a number of photographers are entering the frame laterally. This entry is what is producing a body of work which is removed from the realm of documentary, and it is here that I wish to enter the frame of Mahesh Nair. He is not a"recorder of history" but a passionate producer of images.

While colonial photography has its own singular, unchallenged position as one of the most important records of Indian history, post - independent India saw its own archival recorders in the works of men like Homai Vyrawallah and Kishore Parekh, to name a few. It was Raghu Rai who brought in a singular vocabulary to Indian photography, and others like Dayanita Singh, Ketaki Sheth, Prashant Panjiar and Swapan Parekh added to the discourse.

But when photography started to be challenged and experimented with, painters and photographers started crossing into the geography of painting and superb "new documents" started emerging.

In India photography is still a young medium in comparison to the huge unbroken tradition of fine arts, i.e. painting, sculpture, and printmaking, folk and tribal art. Photography still needs huge amounts of infrastructural support, but within a global context, contemporary Indian photographers are well able to hold their own, particularly in the genre of fashion photography.

A parallel trajectory is seen in documentary photography. Documentary as a language in photography is increasingly gaining visibility within the Indian context. It is the style which is being favoured and showcased by international curators while exhibiting. Indian photography as contemporary Indian art is finding new spaces and global buyers. Yet the very medium of photography lends itself to numerous interpretations and representations.

With the coming of age of photography in India, a new bunch of aware, self confident voices is scanning the drum of image making. Once such visual "document" emerges with the works of Mahesh. He is not simply taking pretty pictures but is investigating the medium; and within the medium, he is refining his technique, his precise gaze and the objectification of representation. Through his own optics he enters into the flora and fauna of surroundings which beckon him, taking with him his constant muse - light. Almost painterly in their presentation, the forests, the water and the mountains which he captures through his lens acquire a life and a beauty of their own.

This was the reason why it became important for Mahesh's work to be read and interpreted through the gaze of the other. Therefore I decided to invite a selection of artists, writers, and thinkers to react to his work. The voices are those which we would call "broad spectrum, and it is these eclectic responses which actually exemplify the connection between image and text, making them both real, individually as well as in totality.

Dr. Alka Pande, currently Consultant Arts Advisor and Curator, Visual Arts Gallery, India Habitat Centre, has been responsible for curating some of Delhi's most unusual and perceptive shows in recent times. Dr Pande is also Visiting Faculty for Aesthetics at the College of Art and formally a Reader, Department of Fine Arts, Punjab University, Chandigarh, with a range of academic papers, lectures and books on the arts to her credit. She has authored several books on art and art history, and has a special interest in ancient Indian erotic literature and art as well as gender and sexuality.

Sonamarg, Kashmir

Tejawas Glacier, Kashmir

Pangong Tso, Ladakh

Pangong Tso, Ladakh

Sarawak, Borneo ▶

lighting up my canvas

paresh maity

Light is the first of painters. There is no object so foul that intense light will not make it beautiful.

– Ralph Waldo Emerson

Light is a magical reality which can be experienced in its numerous *avatars*. From time immemorial, man has been awed and intrigued by light. Whether it be the brilliant striking light from lightning or the subtle glow of the pearl in Vermeer's painting, we tend to pause and marvel at the effects of light.

Artists, especially, have a closer affinity with light. In fact, light and artists work in tandem. Without light in any form of visual art, there would be no art, no visual – and, hence, no meaning. I mean, look at the different play of light in the works of the great masters – mystical in a Rembrandt, beautiful in a Monet and electrifying in a Turner landscape.

Light is an integral part of our world and is universally understood. It sets the mood for any painting. You can say that light is a kind of silent brush that "paints" the surroundings in magical colours. Then the rest is left to the artist's and the viewer's imagination!

Light was the most crucial part of my paintings from the very beginning. I couldn't wait to reach out for my brush and weave in the fascinating colours as I discovered the different ways in which the rays of the morning light fell around me! In fact, my love affair with early morning light began when I was just twelve! Early in the morning, I would wait on the river bank with my colours and brushes in hand and the only subject that I painted was light. It fascinated and tantalized me!

Each artist plays with light in his or her own unique way. I love studying the stark or subtle differences in the result... the splash of colours and illusions created on canvas! One of my great favourites, Rembrandt, was a genius at utilizing light on his canvases three centuries ago! One cannot but marvel at his masterful technique of using different layers of paint so that each layer individually reflected light. This made the final colours look very different from the colours of each layer.

This is so different from the technique used by another of my favourites – Cezanne – especially in his later watercolours. The paintings appear to contain bright sources of light because of his clever exposure of the whiteness of paper in his work. I use this technique a lot in my watercolours, especially when creating the magical effect of shimmering light on the sea or any other water body. You see, white paper is better for creating this effect than white pigment since white pigment is opaque and can never offer the same results! During the early days of my love affair with light in my native Bengal,

I could hardly stop staring in wonderment at the reflection of early morning light on the river. I have a special bond with early morning light; it is what inspires me the most... more than the twilight falling on lush green fields; more than a water-laden sky... and certainly more than the bright sunlight on a clear afternoon.

Early morning light intrigued me as did the whole concept of Impressionism. The whole basis of this movement was for the artist to come out of the closed environment of indoors such as a studio, and come out and capture light and its moments. Thus landscape was my first and foremost expression in water colours, where light was the vital point. How light causes raindrops to glitter like diamonds on the trees after a shower; how the mighty Himalayas change colour many times during the same day or how light makes a chameleon out of nature changing her colours every now and then are very much like a maestro conducting a huge orchestra that makes beautiful music – only, here the maestro is light and one can "see" the music.

Light and shade are the critical ingredients of an artist's expression through any medium – watercolours, sketches, oils or even sculptures. The techniques he or she uses would be very different though, based on the inherent qualities of that medium. Water colours would look lifeless without light. With oils or even sculpture, for that matter, one must work with the reverse technique. One creates the negative (dark) portion first to be able to develop the positive (light).

Every artist has their own preferences in terms of technique and for me that is to use the combined techniques of watercolour and oils even when painting on a canvas. Of course, one must be sensitive to the medium too when going about it. I modify the "white space" technique of watercolours in oils by first painting the entire canvas with a light background colour. Only, the colour I use is a transparent yellow and not white since the colour of light is never white to look at, but has a "see-through" effect because it is a combination of colours.

Generally, no part of my canvas is ever left white. The result is that the colours on the canvas look rich and vibrant. On a canvas, even "dark" has to look transparent. One cannot use black pigment since that will make it look opaque. Darkness is transparent too!

The interplay of light and shade can be utilised in a big way even in a drawing or a sketch. Since a drawing is linear, one has to differentiate the various forms without any tone. The beauty of light and shade is that even using only lines, nearer objects can be accentuated using darker lines and farther objects with lighter lines, naturally using various degrees of shading. It creates the concept of distance and depth and gives an impression of being multi dimensional, even though it is made up of essentially only lines.

Sculpture is a truly multi dimensional medium where shade and light create negative and positive effects respectively.

I am a great admirer of the works of the great sculptor, Henry Moore. His uniqueness lies in the fact that his sculptures are not opaque, they can "breathe" and one can see through large portions of the sculpture! You will notice that his sculptures are full of prominent holes or gaps where your imagination sees the rest.

Speaking of "seeing", an artist's imagination and ability to visualize the effect of light and shadow on an object without looking at it is what differentiates the ordinary from the extraordinary artist. I will share a specific anecdote here of just such an amazing ability. As we know, Leonardo da Vinci was one of the greatest artists that ever lived. He was also a scientist, an architect, an engineer and much more.

Five hundred years ago, the scientist in him made an observation. He said that sunlight reflected from our oceans acts as a secondary light for a crescent moon. At that time nobody had stepped on the moon, there were no satellites and even photography was unknown. Yet, such was his ability to visualize the effect of light and shadow that he created a sketch five hundred years back of this secondary light phenomenon. So vivid was his imagination that when we compare this sketch to an actual photograph taken of the secondary light phenomenon now, it is difficult to believe that he didn't sketch from the photograph!

There is a science in drawing but art cannot be restricted by this science only. It is also about techniques, emotions and imagination. It is, ... well, ... art!

How can I say in words how I feel about light? I can only express it through my work. Mere words cannot do justice to this magical element, for even in the darkness there is light. All we need to do is pause awhile and wait for it to shine through.

Born in Bengal, Paresh Maity graduated in Fine Arts from the Government College of Art & Craft, Calcutta and obtained his Master of Fine Arts from the Delhi College of Art, topping his class. In a short span of twenty years he has held over forty-three solo shows and has participated in several prestigious art camps and group shows in India and outside. He has won acclaim in Europe – particularly in Germany, Switzerland, Hungary, France, United Kingdom and the USA. He has won a number of awards, the most recent being an award from the Royal Watercolour Society, London.

“*Indra*, the God of rain, born of darkness, took the form of light and is fearless like one who has done no wrong and has nothing to hide and so too we all shall remain free of wrong-doing”

Rgveda hymn 3.39.7a, 8a

Leh, Ladakh

Sabah, Borneo

Kaziranga, Assam

Pangong Tso, Ladakh

Nameri, Assam

◄ Nameri, Assam

Pangong Tso, Ladakh ►

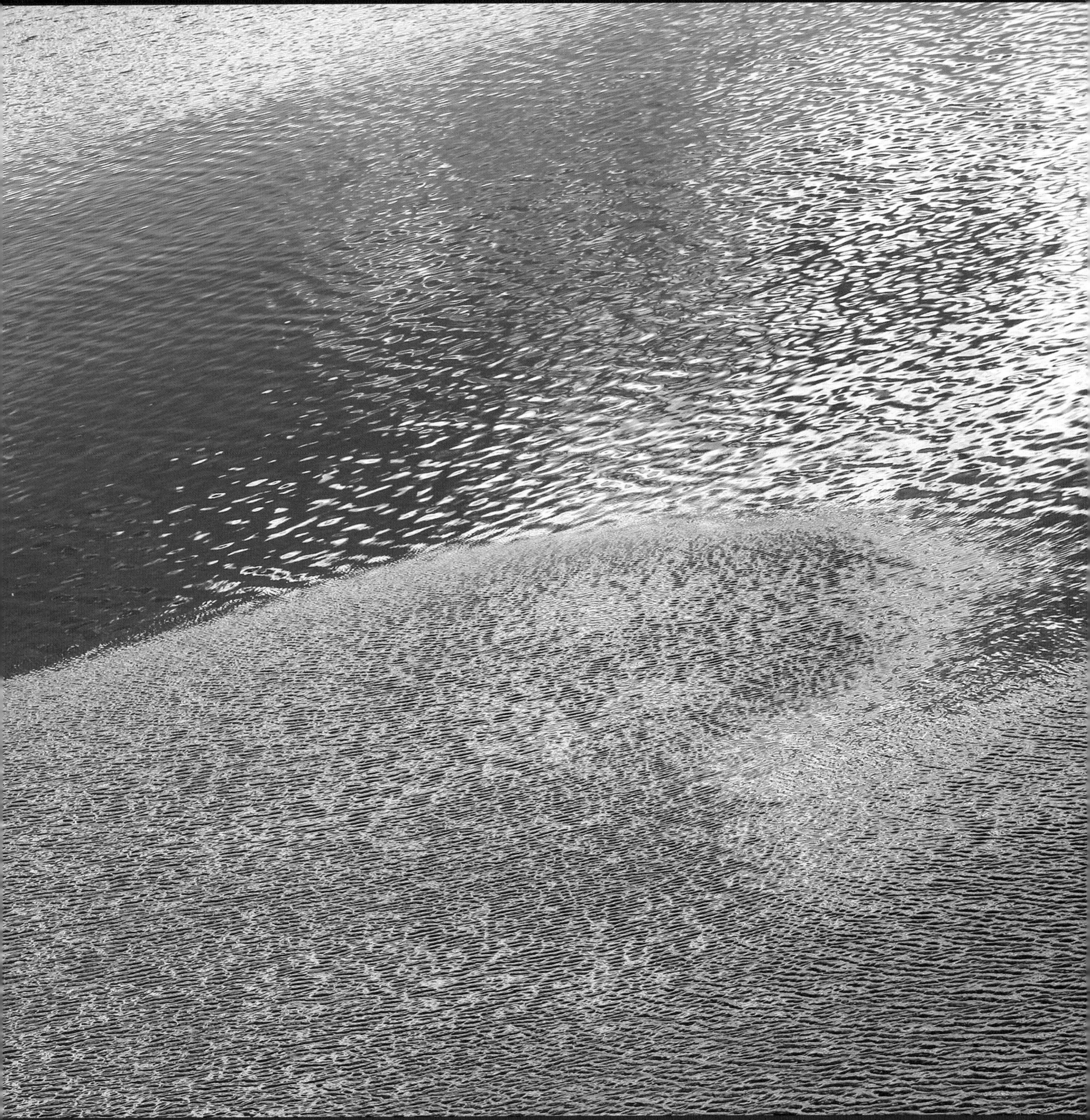

Pangong Tso, Ladakh

Pangong Tso, Ladakh

Pangong Tso, Ladakh

Pangong Tso, Ladakh

Pangong Tso, Ladakh

Pangong Tso, Ladakh

Cumbria, England

Smoo Caves, Scotland

Burren, Ireland

Pangong Tso, Ladakh

Pangong Tso, Ladakh

Pangong Tso, Ladakh

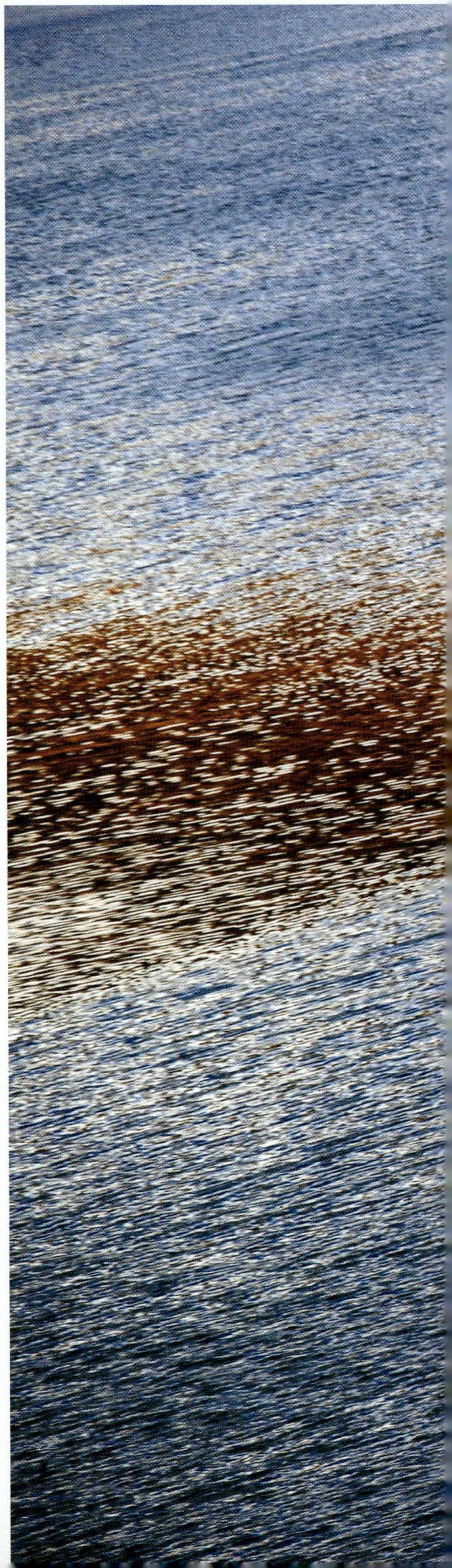

Yellowstone Park, USA

Lusha *Rshi* in his cosmic meditation invokes the gods and prays, "When the day dawn expels darkness, Agni, the God of fire burns, dressing itself in luminosity *(aloka)*. To that vast form, I pray that the earth and the cosmos be caitanya-yukta, become invested with consciousness"

Rgveda hymn 10.35.1b

Yellowstone Park, USA

light and shadows

paulo marcos de moraes

Everything gets frozen in the mountain.
Time becomes eternity.

-Thomas Mann, The Magic Mountain

Photography is one of the most amazing inventions of the 19th century. In 1838, a historian wrote, "Iron, the art of making machines and the art of producing fire and light were instrumental in the emergence of the industrial revolution." The mention of light is a direct reference to chromatography, daguerreotype, photography and kinetoscope.

In fact, one of the greatest discoveries of the most remarkable century of modern times – photography – is due to the physical dimension of light. Photography emerged as a materialization, condensation and precipitation of the imponderable body of light. What photography retains from reality is, as it were, its skeleton... its luminous bone-frame. The reclusive light that hides in the many plaits and sinuosities of the matter is revealed by photography. The photographic image lends weight and figure to the shadow. The double action of light, from the moment of its recording to the development and fixation of images in the darkness of the laboratory, rests on the scientific manipulation of luminous material. It is a matter of assessing how much of the opposites – light and shadow – may be allowed to enter and infiltrate the optical chamber. Not surprisingly, this was magically called *camera obscura* (dark chamber).

The 19th century saw the various stages of chemical imprint evolve – precipitation, filtration, solution. The materials used in the preparation of the plates and in the fixation of the images evoke the procedures and methods of alchemy. Light is, after all, the photographer's raw material. The enterprise of the photographer coincides with that of the alchemist. Their goal is only achieved through transmutation... into light for the photographer and into gold for the alchemist. That is how a whole phantasmagoria was set forth during the 19th century, making each and every photographic work a condensation and projection of light, the "solar gold".

While addressing the chemical origins of photography, Roland Barthes re-emphasizes the idea of a phantasmagoria of light. Thanks to the mediating and mediumistic role of the photo-object, light acts like an "umbilical cord connecting my eyes with the being or the thing already vanished". To Barthes, the photograph in the form of a luminous fragment is what is retained of reality after the latter has vanished away.

The consequent possibility of technical reproducibility of the real world with a "natural" perspective and grandeur represented, in the true sense, a radical cultural revolution. It was also a metaphysical revolution. It signalled the shift from a collective religious mentality to a collective materialistic and laic mentality. Photography imprisons the sunlight,

perpetuates the vanished reality and thereby symbolizes the death of the sacred in the west.

Walter Benjamin, the great visionary who remains relatively unknown even in the west, was a great critic of the process of historical acceleration induced by the advent of technology, later christened as "modernity". He noted that photography constituted a turning point with multiple revolutionary consequences. At least in technical terms, photography clearly outclassed painting as it was able to present the best possible copy of reality.

Claiming to show "life as it is" – as displayed in the propaganda material of the new invention – and not a mere representation of reality, photography played a major role in the attempts to abolish an old dichotomy between facts and representations, which could be traced back to Aristotelian epistemology. However, while digging deep into the matter, Benjamin argues that the metaphysical efforts to overcome the Aristotelian canon proved to be just another form of deception. In the end, photography is nothing but another form of representing reality. The classical axiom remained intact that reality in itself is something inaccessible; the closest we can go to is represent or present it again under a new format, either through language or figuration.

I should reiterate, nevertheless, echoing Benjamin's words, that the emergence of photography (and cinema) as an invention rooted in technology (modernity), had an extraordinary impact. It truly represented a subversion of perspectives with perhaps as much of impact as Renaissance. In fact, Renaissance (re-birth) is a very special period of the history of art. It signals the resumption of something that was dead – the canons of classical Greco-Roman art. In my opinion, the first clear indication of that re-birth was the re-invention or re-discovery of perspective. Though controversies still loom large on the subject, I would dare to point to Giotto as the first artistic genius in whose work one finds clear traces, though rudimentary, of the techniques if not the tricks, aimed at creating an illusion of space and perspective. Giotto resumes the old classical theme of the instrumentation of Euclidean geometry as a means to communicate the ideals of harmony and perfection through painting. In classicist terms, those ideals were conveyed through the juxtaposing and merging of representation and reality.

The case of photography is quite different. Photography was born, primarily, as a technical invention and, above all, as a "machine". Through the camera-machine, perspective presents itself as something readymade; it requires nothing else but an imprint on the celluloid reel. Photography freezes reality in the eternity of the instant – thus its other denomination is "instantaneous".

The socio-cultural events surrounding the new invention are both picturesque and revealing. Contemporary chroniclers report that people flocked from all parts of France and beyond to contemplate for the first time in history the real faces of the celebrities of the world of literature, theatre and politics, which were put on display in the *grand magasins* (the prototype of

today's shopping centres). Till then those faces were just a matter of one's imagination and fancy based on descriptions read in books, magazines and newspapers. In his magnum opus, Walter Benjamin depicts the atmosphere surrounding the first photographic essays (possible only during daylight): "The photographer-scientists would rub shoulders against each another in well-known public spots of Paris, specially in the margins of River Seine, in search of appropriate light; they would spend hours and hours assembling their gadgets which, of course, would often fail to work satisfactorily considering the complex technical, climatic, atmospheric and chemical calculations the new invention involved. A myriad of stunned passersby would gather around those sites and look at the whole technological paraphernalia with a sense of sheer astonishment, as if they were in the presence of a complex astronomic apparatus." Benjamin tells us that even Emperor Napoleon III, after noticing the "black tent" of one of those alchemists in the vicinity of Tuileries, ordered his carriage to stop. He then got down and stood before the camera to be photographed for posterity.

In Brazil, in the last quarter of the 19th century, when photography had already attained maturity, Emperor D. Pedro II, a compulsive self-made scholar known for his commitment to industrial entrepreneurship, sciences and arts, became one of the first photographers in the world. A discreet supporter of modernity, the emperor, a catholic of Habsburg lineage, compiled a hundred of his own photographs till the time of death in his exile in Paris. They stand as a testimony of an excellent technique characterized by classical framing but without failing to reflect the zeifgeist of the new invention (destined, in the opinion of many, to become the successor of painting) in its dealings. With the advent of photography, the masses were brought into the selected realm of art for the first time.

The emergence of photography reflected, therefore, the profound changes taking place in every aspect of human life in its social and cultural dimensions. The primary concern of this article is to highlight the converging and also the conflictive points that conditioned the dialogue with its "rival", the art of painting. Delacroix, undoubtedly the most iconic figure of painting during the romantic 19th century, once stated that he did not believe that a machine could appropriately depict the human face. The following excerpts from the chroniclers of those times (and cited by Walter Benjamin) stand as a clear testimony to the confusion of minds that prevailed in the middle 19th century.

"Humanity has, in fact, created a symbol of remembrance; it invented what seemed to be impossible; it invented a mirror with the power of remembrance. It invented photography... In less than one century, this machine will become the brush, the palette, the colours, the skills, the routine, the patience and the touch of the painter. In less than one century, there won't be any more copyist-painters (maçons en peinture); there will be only architects of painting, painters in the true sense of the term. It's wrong to think that daguerreotype kills art. Not at all; it kills instead the work of patience, the work of time and it pays tribute to thinking. When the

daguerreotype attains the age of maturity, the geniuses of art will take it by the neck and say, "You now belong to me; now, we'll be working together!"

Or, in another context:

"Anyone who has ever put his head under the magic mantle of the photographer, taken a look through the lens and noticed the marvellous reproduction, in miniature, of the natural image..., would have certainly asked himself or herself what will be the destiny of art and specially of modern painting when the photographer succeeds in recording on the plates both the colours and the forms... In fact, the technique and the means of transport introduced by photography diminished the merits of painting as a source of information... Meanwhile, a new reality is in the making; while the daguerreotype appeals to objectivity, painting goes on putting colours as adorning fancies." (Walter Benjamin, in *Paris Capitale du XIX Siecle – Passagenwerk*, pp. 685-699.)

At the end of the day, nobody knows who won and who lost in this debate over painting and photography, which has lasted for over a century. I would venture to say that both won since any attempts to promote a systematic confrontation between art and photography was destined to failure, right from the beginning. The polemic was, after all, an important episode in the general confrontation between art and technique. As time went by, photography became as much a technique, a trade, an industry and a source of entertainment – as a form of art. After the initial defensive reactions by the so-called "colourists" to the perceived threat of the "camera-machine" and, subsequently, the impressionist experiments of Van Gogh and others, painting developed new forms of expression, new methods of utilization of colours, new techniques and new concepts. All in all, it was an amazing revolution that, in the course of time, led to modern and contemporary art.

Thus, beyond the apparent conflict, what has prevailed between photography, painting and also sculpture, is an intense dialogue, an interpenetration of significants and signifiers, an exchange of contents and techniques that has deeply influenced modern art. The amazing impact caused by the instant and sudden materialization of the shadow through the camera-machine was as important to modern art as the technological domestication of light.

Many think that the *chiaroscuro* technique is the child of Italian Renaissance. In reality, the interplay between light and shadow – the dialectics of the sublime – lies in the very origins of mankind and the cosmos. Renaissance was just one of its most intense moments – the climax of dialectics as an aesthetic and metaphysical speculation within the historical development of western art.

Walter Benjamin, the philosopher of the paradox, is perhaps the first to admit that photography, though not eliminating in an ontological sense the duality between appearance and reality, has certainly, in a modern historical sense, rendered that very dichotomy obsolete for all practical purposes. More than that, it has somewhat surpassed reality itself. Through

the power of the image, photography created, so to say, a new reality, a simulacrum of the world. This simulacrum – this kaleidoscope of interpretations – paradoxically became in these times of globalization of images and the advent of "real time", something more than reality or, reality as it can possibly be understood and assimilated by the masses of a "global village".

Artists such as Matisse, Paul Klee Mondrian, who played the role of foundational myths in modern art, showed enough flexibility to incorporate in their works aesthetic elements reflecting the new alchemic power of the negative and the aesthetic attraction for the shadow as an emphasis on light. Matisse stated, "Most of the painters feel the need of direct contact with the objects in order to better experience their existence... they seek an exterior light in order to be able to see things clearly within themselves. Whereas the artist and the poet are endowed with an interior light." (*Writings*, p. 105).

The black and white opposition is described by Klee as "the incessant battle between shadow and light... a movement, a trail covering all locations of the visible till the borders of the invisible." He insists on a "fundamental complementarity between black and white, the two poles around which tonal forces oscillate, creating the equivalent of a musical scale... a scale of colours and notes for the artist to cross all over its extension." (*Theory of Modern Art*, p. 63).

Mondrian considered the dialectical antinomy to be the expression of ancient Christian mysticism. For him "the artist should take the place once reserved for the philosopher and perform the role of a spiritual guide... The battle between light and shadows should allow man, a prisoner of the Platonic cave, to come out in full light... That's the eternal search for equilibrium, for harmony." (*Realist and Surrealist Art*, p. 77).

These western visions are in no way alien to the Hindu tradition. Philosophers like Krishnamurti have stressed that conflict, struggle, and contradiction – the backbone of psychology and human life itself – are a formidable source of existential richness and creativity. The great visionary argued that this embattlement... the inner conflict that translates so often into suffering, was created by the willingness to deny the fact that we are alone; that despite all our "social functions" and status, we are, in fact, alone; we are nothing... but witnesses. In the collective imagination, photography took over the role of witness which had been the prerogative of painting and sculpture for centuries.

I personally believe that art has always been the most eloquent manifestation of one's freedom of consciousness as propounded by Krishnamurti. Since times immemorial, from the prehistoric times of the caverns of Lascaux to the caves of Ajanta and Ellora and the murals of Alchi, art has "worked" its way amidst unavoidable dialectics of conflict or dialectics of the mirror. It has worked hard both in terms of a physical interaction with materials and also in a metaphoric and psycho-spiritual sense of a soul's labour to find its real Self. So, let there be light, but let there also be shadows – from the silver, iced-grey to the heavy dark-plumbeous,... let there be rainbows of shadows!

What stands out in Mahesh's book, with several photographs from Ladakh is the fact that, just like the first scientist-photographers, he works his photographs as if manipulating a mirror. His craft and skills consist of showing us the reflection and the images produced by reality. His approach is very clear. Starting with the locations that he chose for the photographs included in this book, it is a cosmic cradle in which the multiple effects of sunlight on the gigantic mineral and inorganic masses generate amazing organic illusions – textures and forms that soon dissolve once again and evaporate into the golden dust... a sublime farewell of nothingness. Only the silence remains,... the solid silence,... the immeasurable silence – of the rocky plateaus of the Himalayas.

Mahesh's art of photography reaches a culminating point here. The pedagogic humility of the artist and his patient and meticulous mastery of Time – the time of photography,... a time that passes – with all its subtlest nuances – betrays the work of a real painter.... the patient waiting, witnessing and recording of what the cosmic forces "drew" over the primeval canvas. Just like a patient Monet, overlooking his garden of Giverny, Mahesh Nair, tranquil and determined like an orphic guide, takes us by the hand on a visit to the immemorial gallery of the planet. The "Nympheas" de Monet – reflected on the lakes of Pan Gong e Tso Moriri – seems to spring miraculously from his photographs. In the presence of dyed ochres of the huge mountains, wavy and twisted by the light and the shadows, we dream of Leonardo's drawings. Mahesh's journey and dive into the dense and almost inaccessible geography of Ladakh brings back to us the most intimate memories of ourselves. His photographs are paintings of the sublime.

Paulo Marcos de Moraes is a senior diplomat and the current Brazilian Cultural Attaché in New Delhi. He has held several posts prior to this such as the Brazilian Cultural Attaché in Paris, Deputy Director of Brazilian Institute of Research on International Politics and as Vice-President of Brazil-France Foundation, a renowned Museum of Contemporary Art in Rio de Janeiro. He is also the author of many essays published in Brazil on diverse topics, ranging from political philosophy, history, cinema and visual arts.

Burren, Ireland

Glencoe, Scotland

Those who are wise by adoring Usha, the Goddess of Dawn, with hymns of praise become richly endowed with wisdom and *Ushadevi* moves ahead destroying darkness and all wrong-doing. "Your rays,oh goddess, acting like the arms *(bhujayen)* of *Surya* (sun) grant light to all beings."

Rgveda hymns 7.78.3b, 7.79.2d

Leh, Ladakh

Zanskar, Ladakh

Dal Lake, Srinagar

Dal Lake, Srinagar

Silchar Lake, Rajasthan

Pangong Tso, Ladakh

Pangong Tso, Ladakh

Taman Negara, Malaysia ►

Pangong Tso, Ladakh

Nameri, Assam

Pangong Tso, Ladakh

Sarawak, Borneo

Taman Negara, Malaysia

Taman Negara, Malaysia

Munnar, Kerala ►

colour of light

based on inputs from prof. yash pal

Light is the very essence of life; no living being can survive without light in some form. For the common man, light is what our eyes can perceive while a scientist's definition of the phenomenon includes the entire spectrum of electromagnetic radiation. The electromagnetic spectrum extends from radio waves (with wavelengths measuring more than 10,000 kms) to gamma rays (with wavelengths less than 10 trillionths of a metre!). The only difference between the various types of electromagnetic radiation is the amount of energy found in the photons or their wavelength.

As humans, we can perceive only a small fraction of this entire spectrum of electromagnetic radiations that we call "visible light". Visible light – that which can be seen with our eyes – constitutes less than a millionth of one percent of the total electromagnetic spectrum!

Light has fascinated and inspired creative people – poets, artists, photographers – for ages and their handiwork is there for all to see. Yet, over the centuries its multiple and diverse characteristics have also engrossed scientists. Initially scientists debated over whether light was a wave or was it composed of particles? Only much later did Einstein prove the duality of light. It is a stream of photon particles and it is a rippling motion of pure energy waves through space. It is this dichotomy that makes the study of light so interesting.

The sun is the main source of light for all creatures on Earth. Its surface temperature is about 5800 degrees celsius, while its core is over 10 million degrees Celsius! Although light travels at a phenomenal speed (approximately 186,000 miles per second or 300,000,000 metres per second), it still takes eight minutes for the rays of the sun to reach us!

To appreciate what this means, consider this – what we see as the Andromeda Galaxy is not the Andromeda as exists today. In fact, what we see is the way the Andromeda Galaxy was 2 million years ago, which is how long it takes light to reach the earth from there! For all we know, at this moment as you read this, Andromeda Galaxy may not exist any more; but we will find out only two million years later!

That brings me to yet another unique property of light – its speed. The Special Theory of Relativity states that nothing can travel faster than the speed of light. In the last century, Einstein's abstract theory and equations have been proven true. Now even science fiction authors talk about the "hyperjump" as a means for us to travel vast distances in space.

No matter how impressive these statistics might sound, most of us are moved not by the chemistry of light but by the small visible part of the spectrum – the light that creates what we call beauty. Whether it is as innocuous as the bright red on a flower, the green on a bird or the truly awesome phenomenon called the Aurora Borealis, it makes us pause, wonder and admire.

Almost all of us carry childhood memories of spotting the first rainbow in the sky. Rainbows, in fact, have fascinated humans since time immemorial and as such, have been the subject of

songs, poems, stories and mythology. In Norse mythology, it was believed to be the road connecting the world of the gods to the world of men; for the Greeks it was a sign from the gods foretelling war or heavy rain. The Indians saw it as the bridge between life and death and the Irish believed in the famous pot of gold that lay at the end of the rainbow.

But not many of us notice that whenever we admire a rainbow in front of us, the sun is *always* behind us. Actually, the rainbow we see is created by thousands of water droplets that act like tiny prisms enabling us to see the individual component colours of white light (sunlight). Each falling raindrop flashes the colours to the observer for just an instant before another drop takes its place. A quick succession of flashing colours results in the impression of a static view of a colourful arch across the sky. However, for this to happen the sun must be behind us in the sky; rainbows can never be created or seen when the sun is directly overhead.

Also, the rainbow is light reflected to the eye at a specific angle of 42 degrees to the original ray of sunlight as measured from each observer's eye. In other words, no two persons see exactly the same rainbow!

That is not all. Although the rainbow looks like a bow or an arc, it is actually a circle. Water droplets refract the light from the sun over an angle of about 42 degrees. This angle is so big that the rainbow appears centred on a point opposite the sun called the anti-solar point, and seems to form around it. The bow shape is, therefore, only a part of a circle of light, while the rest is cut off by the horizon obstructing it. The lower the sun is in the sky the larger is the arch that it forms, and consequently, the more visible it is. At higher altitudes, it is possible to see the full circle of a rainbow. The horizon does not block our line of sight when we are flying in an aeroplane at a high altitude.

That was all about the Primary Rainbow. But perhaps you have sometimes noticed the Secondary Rainbow as well? This is another, larger rainbow that is often seen running parallel to the primary rainbow and creating the impression of a double rainbow. The secondary rainbow is created in a manner similar to the primary rainbow, except that in this case, the sun's light is reflected twice internally before it emerges from the water droplet (raindrop). As a result, the sequence of colours that we see are reversed. That is also the reason why colours in the secondary rainbow are never as bright as those in the primary rainbow.

Like in the case of the rainbow, all the brilliant colours that we perceive around us are the result of just two properties of light – reflection and refraction. But how does it all happen? The answer is as fascinating as the question itself.

Visible light has an entire range of frequencies. When it falls on matter around us, certain specific frequencies get absorbed while the rest are either transmitted or reflected. The colour that we perceive with our eyes is actually the colour of light that is reflected or transmitted by those objects. Green leaves contain chlorophyll molecules that absorb almost all other frequencies of visible light, except green, and therefore green is the colour reflected back to us. When all the frequencies are absorbed we see the colour black and when all of them are reflected, the eye perceive the object to be white.

So why is the sky blue? A clear, cloudless, day-time sky is blue because molecules in the air scatter the blue light coming from the sun which has a shorter wavelength as compared to the longer wavelength red light. Here is a puzzle - if shorter wavelengths are scattered more strongly, then why is the sky not violet, the colour of light with the shortest visible wavelength? The answer to this is that the spectrum of light emitted from the sun is not constant for all wavelengths and much of it is absorbed by the high atmosphere. Also, our eyes are less sensitive to the colour violet. So, blue is what we see.

However, since a rainbow shows that a significant amount of visible light coloured indigo and violet remain beyond the blue, this explanation is only a part of the answer. The remaining answer to the puzzle lies in the way our vision works. Human beings have three types of colour receptors, or cones, in our retina. These are called red, blue and green because they respond most strongly to light of these respective colours (wavelengths). As they are stimulated in different proportions, our visual system constructs the colours we see, regardless of whether they actually occur in nature in the same mathematical proportion or not.

When we look up at the sky, the red cones respond to the small amount of scattered red light, and less strongly to the orange and yellow wavelengths. Green cones respond to yellow light and the more strongly scattered green and green-blue wavelengths. Blue cones are stimulated by colours near the blue wavelengths that are scattered very strongly. If there were no indigo and violet in the spectrum, the sky would appear to be blue with a slight green tinge. However, the most strongly scattered indigo and violet wavelengths stimulate the red as well as the blue cones slightly, which is why these colours appear blue with an added red tinge.

The net effect is that the red and green cones are stimulated by the light from the sky almost equally while the blue is stimulated more strongly. This combination accounts for the pale blue colour of the sky. It may not be just a coincidence that our vision is adjusted to see the sky as a pure hue. Over time human beings have evolved to fit in with their environment to the maximum possible degree, and the ability to separate natural colours clearly is probably a survival advantage.

When we look towards the sun at sunset, we see red and orange colours simply because the blue light has been scattered out and away from our line of sight. Sunsets are reddened because when the sun's position is very low or just below the horizon, the light passing at grazing incidence upon the earth must pass through a greater thickness of air than when it is overhead. Just before the sun disappears from view,

its actual position is about a diameter below the horizon, the light having been bent by refraction to reach our eyes. Since short wavelengths are more efficiently scattered (by Rayleigh scattering), more of them are scattered out of the beam of sunlight before it reaches you. An equivalent phenomenon can be seen at sunrise.

But did you know that just as the sun goes down over the horizon, there is a green flash that lasts for a few seconds? The green flash is an atmospheric refractive phenomenon where the top edge of the sun turns green momentarily. It is rarely seen by the naked eye, primarily because it requires specific conditions to occur, and also because it requires the observer to know exactly what to look for. Contrary to its name which is completely misleading, there is no actual "flash". To add to the elusiveness of the phenomenon, it lasts for only about a fraction of a second or, at most, for a few seconds.

The cause for the green flash is the bending of the sun's rays by refraction. The atmosphere acts like a weak prism, separating the light into different colours. Blue light is bent more than red light. However, the amount of refraction even at the horizon is quite small – only a few seconds of arc (one second of arc is $1/3600^{th}$ of a degree). This effect is magnified by the atmosphere itself. Layering in the atmosphere causes an effect similar to a horizontal cylindrical lens; the separation of the colour bands is exaggerated in the vertical direction, and can last up to several minutes of arc (one minute of arc is $1/60^{th}$ of a degree).

One may ask what conditions are required to see the green flash? The green flash is best observed when you have a clear view of the horizon uncluttered by foreground objects and when the atmosphere is pollution free. This usually means that you need to see a distance of several miles "out", almost to the point where the curvature of the earth defines the limit. This is probably why stories of seeing the green flash frequently occur when at the ocean, since at such locations one is looking at the horizon through an additional amount of atmosphere when the sun sets. Equally important is the fact that in the ocean the line of vision is nearly parallel to the horizon.

So then why is it called a "green" flash and not a "blue" flash? The reason for this is that contamination in the atmosphere scatters blue light and removes it from the line of sight. Consequently, more green light gets through and is therefore seen more clearly. However, under extraordinary conditions, a "blue" flash might also be seen.

The secrets of light and colour are a fascinating, never-ending discovery. What we know today is just a fraction, a mere glimpse of the knowledge waiting to be discovered. Our understanding of light continues to evolve. Already, researchers have created pulses of light that contains photons that do not travel! Similarly, can you imagine "solid light"? It is almost a certainty that a thousand years later, what we consider knowledge today might be looked upon as a myth of a bygone era. Strange as it might seem today, not so long ago we believed that our earth was flat!

As new vistas of knowledge emerge, perhaps the best thing to do would be to look around and absorb the marvels of colours and light in all their splendour, as they surround us with their magic of everyday occurrence and existence.

Professor Yash Pal is probably one of India's most widely known scientific names. A well-known astrophysicist, he is the man responsible for setting up the first satellite education system in the country. Scientist, teacher, author and philosopher, Professor Pal has been associated with Tata Institute of Fundamental Research (TIFR), Massachusetts Institute of Technology (MIT), Neils Bohr Institute and Indian Space Research Organisation – to name just a few of the hundreds of organizations and initiatives that he has been associated with over the last six decades. In 1976, Professor Pal was awarded the Padma Bhushan by the Government of India for his contribution to Science and Space Technology.

Sonamarg, Kashmir

Zanskar, Ladakh ►

Kargil, Ladakh

Zanskar, Ladakh

Zanskar, Ladakh

Gulmarg, Kashmir

◄ Leh, Ladakh

In an extended meditation on the Sun, Vibhrata *Rshi* adores him as "The shining source of all food, as the first among the luminous ones, as one who is always moving into the illumined part of the sky, the support of all noble acts and as the regenerator of all the worlds".

Rgveda hymn 1.170.2 – 4

Kargil, Ladakh

Zanskar, Ladakh

Darchik, Ladakh

Glencoe, Scotland ►

"Even *soma*, the fabled, auspicious inebriating drink is *diptimana*, marked by the shining of light" sings *Rshi* Nrimedha, son of Angira. "The light that *soma* donates to the day had protected Manu the *Rajarshi* by lending its power to the all-destroying *Asura*."

Rgveda hymns 9.29.2c ,9.92.5c

Darchik, Ladakh

Leh, Ladakh

◄ Leh, Ladakh

Leh, Ladakh

Leh, Ladakh

Leh, Ladakh ►

Pangong Tso, Ladakh

Zanskar, Ladakh

Kargil, Ladakh

Dras, Ladakh

Rangdum, Ladakh

Rangdum, Ladakh

light up my life

dr. naveen sakhuja

Many millennia ago when God said, "Let there be light", I don't think even He realized the gravity of those words! Of all our senses, there is none more important than sight. It is God's most fascinating creation to date and possibly His most complicated and successful one in the animal world.

Vision in animals

Speaking of animals, the ability to perceive light greatly varies from creature to creature depending on its need for survival. Bees, for example, can see ultraviolet rays. As a result, certain flowers that have an ultraviolet hue – not perceived by humans – attract them. However, they cannot see the red end of the spectrum. Reds appear black to them.

Snakes, on the other hand, have no use for ultraviolet vision and have infrared (heat rays) vision instead. This helps them locate warm-blooded prey. Certain pit vipers can detect temperature changes up to milli-kelvins! An interesting aside here is that the army also uses this mechanism in infrared goggles.

The eyes of most birds are on either side of their heads. This placement allows them to see things on each side as well as in front of them at the same time. This type of vision is called *monocular vision.* Birds with eyes placed like this get a wide area of vision that enables them to sense danger quickly. For instance, pigeons can see about 300 degrees without turning their heads. Some birds like woodcocks have their eyes placed far back on the sides of their heads, allowing them an even greater range to be able to detect danger behind them. However, birds with monocular vision have a harder time judging distances and have bad perception of depth.

The type of vision that occurs when the field of vision from each eye overlaps is called *binocular vision.* Birds such as hawks have their eyes placed far to the front giving them binocular vision, like human beings. These birds may have a 180 degree field of overall vision with much of that being binocular. Their frontal vision is much sharper than that of their monocular cousins. Doves, for instance, only have 30 degrees of binocular vision.

Owls have wonderful binocular vision and make up for the lack of lower field of vision by an amazing ability to turn their heads to face backwards. Though the structure of a bird's eye is similar to that of humans in many ways, there are some very important differences. Most birds' eyes are flatter than human eyes – a feature that allows them to have a larger area in focus at any given time. In contrast, humans can focus on smaller areas at a time. Also, unlike in humans, the eyes of most birds do not move in their sockets. Instead, reflex movements of their necks usually replace eye movements.

Structure of the eye

The eye – only 25 mm in diameter – is as complex as anything can possibly be. No camera manufacturer has designed such a feature-packed camera of this size with longevity that matches that of the owner's! Light is focused through a complex mechanism, much akin to an auto-focus camera but infinitely more sensitive, many times faster and far more responsive.

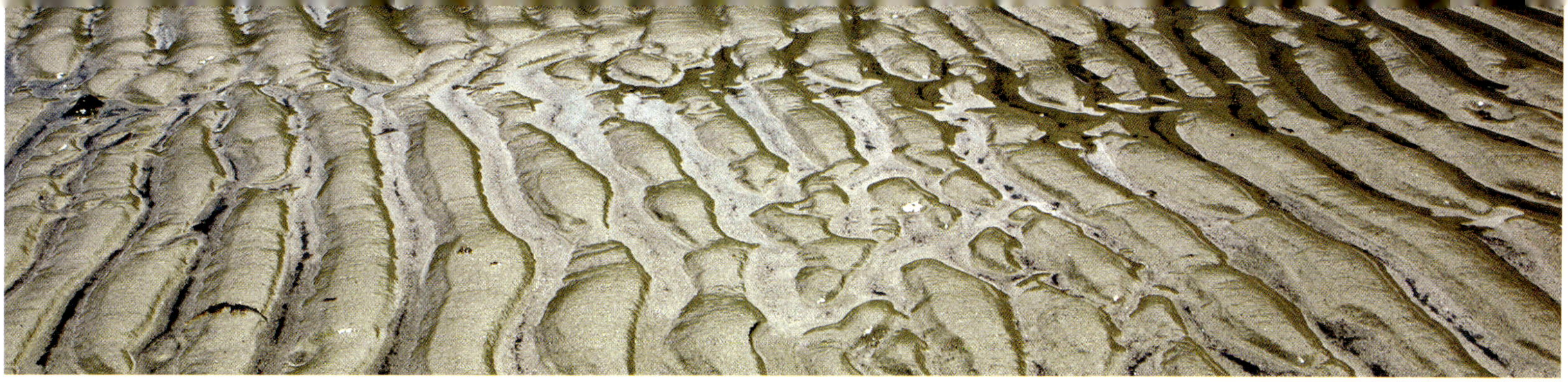

Focusing is done by a dual lens system – the cornea and the crystalline lens.

The cornea, with a power of approximately +42-45 dioptres, is the watch-glass like structure on which people wear their contact lenses. The partially focused rays are further focused by the crystalline lens, which has a power of approximately +21.00 dioptres. This complex system brings light to a focus on the retina. People who cannot focus on the retina need glasses to help them achieve this focus.

The lens has the inherent ability to alter its power, even though this ability to change its focus diminishes with age... That is why people usually start needing glasses as they grow older. The range of the lens can be as much as +16.00 dioptres during childhood, When this lens becomes opaque it is referred to as a cataract.

If the eye were a camera, the retina would be the film. In the centre of the retina there is a circular area called the fovea centralis. This has the highest level of sensitivity to light. Although it is only 0.6 mm in diameter (about the size of a dot created with a sharp pencil), it contains the densest concentration of photoreceptors.

Photoreceptors are highly specialized cells that detect light and then convert the light energy into electrical energy. There are essentially two types of photoreceptors in the retina – rods and cones. Rods are active in low light and good for perceiving motion and they essentially show shades of grey. They are used maximally in night or twilight vision. The retinal pigment is made of Vitamin A.

As for the cones, they are of 3 types – red, blue and green. These are the primary colours. The cone cells detect the primary colours and the brain mixes them in infinitely variable proportions so that we can perceive a wide range of colours. Prolonged exposure to colours can cause fatigue in the cone cells. This changes the manner in which one perceives the colour of the object that one is viewing.

There are much fewer cone cells than rod cells in the retina. Also, many animals do not have cone cells and hence do not see in colour. The maximum concentration of cones is in the fovea, which is why it is the most sensitive area of the retina. The human eye features a wavelength response from around 400 to 700 nanometres, with peak sensitivity at 555 nanometers (in the green region of the visible light spectrum) when fully adapted to light. This should explain why the grass is greener on the other side! It might also explain the colour of money!!

Malfunctions in our little camera

The human eye – this complicated little camera, can also malfunction occasionally. Almost all of us suffer from the dread of having to lose our sight and even a little alteration in the quality of our vision causes us enormous worry. Yet, it can have some very off-beat implications, especially for the works of some of the great masters! For instance, given the multiplicity of diagnoses, it is not clear if Van Gogh suffered from a visual disorder and if so, what its origins were.

Van Gogh - The well-known doctor, Paul-Ferdinand Gachet, a physician for one of the France's railroad companies, treated Van Gogh with digitalis, possibly for mania and/or epilepsy. In the 19th century, digitalis, extracted from the purple foxglove plant, was one of the main treatments for these disorders. It was used as a sedative, an anticonvulsant and an anti-manic agent. One of the side effects of systemic digitalis treatment is a disturbance in yellow-blue vision (xanthopsia) that is similar to viewing the world through a yellow filter. Glare and coloured haloes may also be experienced as visual side effects.

Many of Van Gogh's works – *The Starry Night, The Night Café, Sunflowers* and his later self-portraits – all have a distinctive yellow hue. The yellow tone is especially noticeable in the stars in *The Starry Night*, in *Enclosed Field with Reaper* and in Van Gogh's flesh in his self-portrait dedicated to Paul Gauguin. It is possible that digitalis-induced xanthopsia was making Van Gogh perceive the world with a yellow tint. The predominance of coloured halos around light sources in various works, such as *The Starry Night*, may also be attributable to the effects of digitalis.

Alternatively, it has been proposed that the haloes in Van Gogh's works are due to a form of glaucoma. The elevation in intraocular pressure associated with glaucoma can lead to corneal oedema (swelling). The swollen cornea diffracts light into its component parts, causing the observer to perceive coloured haloes around light sources. Since glaucoma is rarely seen among individuals below the age of forty, it is unlikely that Van Gogh, who died at thirty-seven, was so afflicted.

There are alternative explanations for the over-abundance of yellow in Van Gogh's work. He was fascinated with colour and its effects and often experimented with different ranges of tone as well as with different styles and palettes to suit each painting. Interestingly, while the effects of xanthopsia should have minimized the amount of blue in his work, in most of his paintings there is a strong presence of blue tones. In his correspondence, he often wrote about the importance of a balance between yellow and blue in his work. Of course, considering that haloes have been painted historically to create atmosphere, mood, and symbolism, it is quite possible that Van Gogh's haloes may also have been painted for the same reasons and is present as a part of his artistic style.

Rembrandt - Although there is no documented evidence regarding changes in Rembrandt's vision, certain changes in his work may well be the result of visual aging, while others may be the result of purposeful stylistic change. Rembrandt's earlier works show him to be a master of detail and light sensitivity. In visual terms, this means that he had good acuity and contrast sensitivity, which appeared to decline as he aged. Certainly, he experienced the universal age-related loss of the ability to focus on near stimuli, (presbyopia). This would have made it more difficult to engage effectively in near range visual tasks such as painting.

It is also possible that in his later years, Rembrandt experienced visual loss caused by an age-related opacity of the lens of his eye (cataract). Whatever the cause, notable visual changes appear to characterize Rembrandt's later works. They appear to be reduced in detail, clarity and light sensitivity. The fine brush strokes and careful precision that are evident in his early work, gave way to work that was loose, heavy, and less clearly defined.

Monet - Monet wrote of his growing frustration with his deteriorating vision, describing how he was forced to memorize where the colours were placed on his palette. In 1914 he wrote in his correspondence that colours no longer had the same intensity. He complained that his reds had begun to look muddy and that his paintings looked more and more darkened. He was forced to rely on the labels on the tubes of paint in place of his own vision. Slowly, progressive age-related cataracts manifest as yellowing and darkening of the lens. After reluctantly submitting to cataract surgery in 1923, Monet returned to his original painting style, throwing away much of the artwork that he had done during the ten-year period that he had been afflicted by cataract.

Size does matter

There are millions... yes, millions... of microscopic nerves that carry miniscule impulses of broken-up images to the brain within nanoseconds. The brain then analyses these electrical impulses and "joins" them to make the big picture. It tells you the colour, size and orientation of the perceived object and also assesses the distance, size of the object and speed at which it is approaching you or receding from you. In addition,

if it perceives a threat, it sends instant impulses to the head, neck and eyelids. All the while that this is happening, fresh impulses are being sent in nanoseconds! Makes you want to change your computer, doesn't it?

I want to admit something that I don't normally do. Some fifteen years have passed since I finished my formal education. During this time I have begun to strut and brag a little less about how good I am at my job. Now I think more and more that I don't seem to know as much as I would have liked to and I am becoming increasingly convinced that God is on my side. I feel that I'm more lucky than brilliant because the product (the human eye) is so outstanding that it rarely requires serious repair and has a terrific shelf life, despite being used 24x7 – yes, even during sleep... remember those dreams???

The few aspects of sight restoration that technology has allowed us to rectify are extremely gratifying. Without any bias, I truly believe that there is no surgery more gratifying than eye surgery. The results are instantaneous, with the patient being able to see almost immediately after the surgery. Even after so many years, it still gives me a thrill and a high when I see the expression and sheer happiness on the face of a person whose sight has been restored. To illustratrate what sight means to us and how it affects our thinking, I will relate a little story that is absolutely true.

About fifteen years ago, a few of us went to one of the interior villages to conduct an eye camp. There were four surgeons, nurses, OT technicians and others. We lived on the hospitality of the villagers for ten days and were treated like kings. During this period we must have operated on over 150 cases, one of which is particularly difficult to forget.

On the second day of the camp, a family brought their aging patriarch to me for surgery. The old man was totally blind with cataracts in both eyes. He was operated upon successfully the next day and his bandages were opened the day after that. All through, a little boy sat with him and spent the nights too with him at the camp. When the bandage was finally opened, the old man could barely open his eyes, as he was not used to the gush of light that he was now exposed to. The first thing he asked for was to see the little boy who rushed to his side. On seeing him the old man remarked that the boy seemed smaller than what he remembered. He was then gently told that this was his great-grandson and not his grandson whom he had last seen before the lights went out.

"Radiant, shine, lustre, brilliant, vivid, glare, blaze, beam, gleam, glade, flare, glimmer, shimmer, twinkle, sparkle, glisten, glitter, reflect, daylight, moonlight, twilight, dawn, sunrise, sunset, noon, moonbeam, luminescence, fluorescence, halo, nimbus, aurora, polar lights, lightning, thunderbolt, candlelight, midnight oil, limelight, spotlight, optics, beacon, spangle, flicker, ..."

Such words would have no meaning had it not been for a tiny part of us measuring only one inch in diameter. It is a sensory device that we have much to be grateful for. This outstanding series of images by Mahesh goes a long way to further emphasize this very fact!

Rshi Brhaddiva says "One from whom the light-permeated sun emanated is primary, supreme – there was nothing before Him. The God Vena was infiltrated with light. He the maker of water blesses the earth by showering sun-progeny rain from the heart of the sky. When the sun and water meet and mingle, the wise, prayerful ones – like children – praise and please Vena with sweet, happy words."

Rgveda hymns10.120.1a,10.123.1b

Dr. Navin Sakhuja is a practising Ophthalmologist and is now in private practice in New Delhi. He is also a keen photographer whose interest in photography started in 1989 and is now a passion. He finds time to pursue both, his profession and passion with equal zeal. He believes that both ophthalmology and photography require total commitment, perfection, attention to detail and are all about perceiving light in the best way possible and feels blessed that he has been given the chance to pursue both.

Zanskar, Ladakh

Zanskar, Ladakh

Zanskar, Ladakh

◄ Zanskar, Ladakh

Leh, Ladakh

◄ Zanskar, Ladakh

Zanskar, Ladakh

Zanskar, Ladakh

Kargil, Ladakh

Leh, Ladakh

Leh, Ladakh

Kargil, Ladakh

Leh, Ladakh

Kargil, Ladakh

Leh, Ladakh

Leh, Ladakh

Kargil, Ladakh

Zanskar, Ladakh

Darchik, Ladakh

Darchik, Ladakh

Leh, Ladakh

Leh, Ladakh

Pangong Tso, Ladakh

Leh, Ladakh ►

Leh, Ladakh

Pangong Tso, Ladakh

Pangong Tso, Ladakh

Leh, Ladakh

the zen in light

santosh sivan

Our world is made of light...

Its tenderness can kindle a romance and its harshness can crack the earth. It can violently force its way through as shafts and it can gently spread itself like the caress of a lover. Its touch can turn oceans into gold and its warmth can wake up the earth. Its cover turns into the coolness of the moon and its play gives us night and day. Its motion causes seasons and its harmony is enlightenment. From its form we are born and into it we decline.

This is light – the power of the sun as I appreciate it in nature. It conditions the way we see the world, it stimulates our senses and it shapes our responses to visuals. It continuously evolves, revealing moods and emotions. With its metamorphosis it unfolds unto us forms, shapes, textures and colours. The more we are in synergy with light, the more it sharpens our understanding of the environment and how we perceive beauty and form.

My attempts to capture light are based on my experiences with the weather – the rain, the sun, the snow and the clouds. In Kerala, where I grew up, heavy monsoon rains were a part of our lives. There was water everywhere – in the rain, the pond, the sea and the backwaters. Fascination for water honed my eye for colour and light. As children, when we set out to play hockey, my friends would ask, "Will it rain today? Should we go to the grounds?" I would stand on my terrace and say, "It will clear up in one minute" or "It will rain after half an hour." Soon I became an expert at this and realized that I could predict the weather with reasonable accuracy.

Also, while watching the clouds build up and disappear, I noticed different shades of green and blue. Some plants looked different against a particular shade of blue and a particular type of cloud highlighted the green to a striking colour. The sun would burst in after a quick shower and light up the whole formation. Or it would bring out a new freshness in the green. I began to understand nature and its attributes and the beauty of change. These moments of light and colour were magic.

Beauty at its best can be caught in a fleeting moment. The fading away of an evening into the night or the sun breaking at dawn are enchanting flights of time. They need to be snapped up fast. Maybe that is why I work swiftly – to capture the maximum change possible. When Keralites watched the ad films that I made for the state's tourism board, they told me that they had never seen their region like that before. Yet, all I had tried to do was to capture the changes in nature.

When we venture into the world of visuals we enter a world where moments are discovered and preserved in their original essence. In each thing around us, there is a hidden photograph waiting for that one right look to reveal itself. While good pictures wait to be discovered, experiment and exploration lead a photographer to break new ground; composition, lighting and most importantly timing, are a part of the game. Be it a crowded street, a desert, a beach or a factory, the camera makes its presence felt.

Cinematography is an extension of photography. It involves the same essentials, except that the image here is moving and is the combined effort of the director, the actors and the lensman. A photographer can graduate to a cinematographer because his basic senses are in tune with the visual world.

A cinematographer determines how people respond to a film visually and collaborates with the director to search for the right look and spaces. Like a director, each of us seeks a unique way of expressing what we are looking for. But the bottom line for a cinematographer is to translate the director's vision into a visual.

I respect and admire earlier generations of cinematographers. They laid the foundation for us to see the world poetically and to learn the dance of light and shadow. One can learn from books and guides but experimenting is the only way to realize one's potential. To me, visual art is best learnt through a journey of self-discovery – with light and visuals guiding one's passion.

If an idea has to be conveyed emphatically, nothing should cross its path. The entire exercise of making a film needs that special energy. Eventually it becomes an extension of your soul. Locations are where ideas are given form – where a scene is visualized before it is filmed. The strangeness of any new location sets my thoughts in motion – to understand it, to accept it and to breed a familiarity. Thus, I know the hostility of snow, the fury of rains and the fragility of sunset. A cinematographer will wait for nature to clear or wax in a certain way.

Cinematography has some ground-zero principles. You do not need various accessories for great work to happen. Make it happen with whatever you have. Being technically advanced is different from being a slave to accessories.

In feature films, the script and the dialogue set the mood. Still, sometimes you can get the visuals to speak for themselves, especially in documentaries, where during filming visual moments get captured. In a feature film, the emphasis may lie elsewhere. Sometimes, we try to combine the finesse of an art film and the extravaganza of mainstream commercial cinema – a little bit of Zen and a little bit of Sin.

Any human face is a study. Focusing on a face can underline the way she breathes or how his brows twitch. But it is more interesting if you focus beyond the face – into the mind and into its thought and feeling. Close-ups enhance perspectives and give a different meaning to sound. In *The Terrorist*, water was studied closely. Throughout the film, there is a parallel between the aquatic elements and the protagonist's state of mind; the water fluctuates from a drop to a trickle to a ripple.

I am lucky to have been born and brought up in Kerala, a region with a rich visual language. The colour geography of Loyola School in Thiruvananthapuram, where I studied, was very interesting. Everything – the blackboard, the chalk, the pencil, the paper, the priests' attire and the school uniform

– had a black and white quality to it. From Loyola, I would be taken to my grandfather's house in Haripad, a centre of culture with ten-day festivals, elephants bathing, lush green backwaters and a whole visual culture of art forms like kathakali and theyyam. For someone coming from a black and white world, it was a burst of colours that touched me.

In Haripad, I spent time with my grandmother, who sketched and narrated tales of good winning over evil: of how yakshis and ghosts wearing old-fashioned clothes appeared on moonlit nights, with smiles that created fear. I thought and imagined their façade even in my sleep. These were probably the first visuals that I imagined... the kind of things that one had heard of but not seen in real life. In school, I read *Jungle Picture* by Norah Burke. The story *Blue Bead* sparked visual images of a girl and her relationship with nature. She thinks that the pond is her best friend – she can see the weeds, the fish, the birds and herself in it. It triggered a visual poem of all the dew drops coming together and then, when the sun comes out, the dew drops turning into a pond. The blue bead is the elusive bead that she wants for the prime position in the necklace that she is making from different stones in the jungle. Here, sunlight takes a violent form and reaches into the jungle as shafts. I made it into the film *Malli.*

Sometimes, a specific moment can change the ordinary into something special – something with meaning. And capturing it makes you feel good. We tend to take existence for granted. When we are no more, the sun and the moon will still rise. We liked to look at them and we will never see them again.

In *Asoka*, one of the greatest moments was Shah Rukh Khan walking into the frame where I could shoot a scene with the sun going down and the moon rising. In a battlefield, with people struck down, it means only one thing... everything, including life, is fleeting. There is nothing that anyone can conquer. You can buy a house or a piece of land and say, "This is mine." But you belong to it for just a tiny bit of time. That's the Zen.

Santosh Sivan grew up in the city of Thiruvananthapuram (Trivandrum) in Kerala, India, where he attended Loyola School and Mar Ivanios College. His father, Sivan, is a renowned director and cinematographer of Malayalam documentary films and runs the Trivandrum-based Sivan Studio. Sivan graduated from the Film and Television Institute of India in 1984. In December 1995 he became a founding member of the Indian Society of Cinematographers (ISC). A noted cinematographer, Sivan won eleven National Film Awards from his participation as a cinematographer in over forty films from the 1980s to mid-1990s. His success as a director began with his critically acclaimed The Terrorist in 1999. He solidified his reputation with the release of Asoka in 2001.

Srinagar, Kashmir

Junagadh, Gujarat

Junagadh, Gujarat

Nalsarovar, Gujarat

Junagadh, Gujarat

Taman Negara, Malaysia

Kaziranga, Assam

Kaziranga, Assam

Binsar, Uttaranchal ►

Binsar, Uttaranchal

Taman Negara, Malaysia

Ranthambore, Rajasthan

Another sage adores *Usha*, the Goddess of dawn, for inspiring *jyoti* in the vast sky and become the source of *anna*, food. "*Svarga-putri*, the daughter of heaven, enveloped by effulgence *(jyoti)* gradually begins to be seen in the east as if reading the mind of Sun. She traverses the same path as he and permeates all directions."

Rgveda hymn 1.92.17b, 1.124.3b

Rangdum, Ladakh

Pangong Tso, Ladakh

Hawkshead, England

Rangdum, Ladakh

Nalsarovar, Gujarat

Agatti, Lakshadweep

cosmic dance

lakshmi vishwanathan

Innocence is like the subtle light of dawn. That is the state of mind a child has when she learns her first steps of dance – "*theyya, theyyi*". Her body reflects the way she feels; her mind has no inhibitions and seems ready for an adventure. The rhythm of dance energizes the young body and brings the lightness of joy in the playful tapping of the feet. Later, more geometrical movements follow when the arms sweep, making straight lines, triangles, circles and squares. Knees bend and the torso brings into shape not only the beautiful curves of the body, but also angles of varying degrees. Within vast, ever-changing permutations and combinations of rhythms and lines, colour seeps in gently. First, it is just a touch of the finger, the bending of a wrist or the flexing of a muscle. But soon the colours deepen in shade and richness. The narrative of dance takes over. Now the movements have meaning. They establish character. Gradually they unfold stories, situations and the essential dramatic moods in dance – the *Nava Rasa* or the nine Rasas.

The nine Rasas – *shringara* (love), *hasya* (laughter, comic), *karuna* (sadness, pathos), *raudra* (fury, anger), *vira* (heroic, pride), *bhayanaka* (terrible, fear), *bibhatsa* (disgust), *adbhuta* (awe-inspiring, marvellous) and *shanta* (peaceful) – colour the landscape of dance as if the different moods are caused by the periodic play of light and shade from dawn to dusk. The beauty of these moods in dance is that unlike in a picture or a painting, dance can create a magical, meaningful, lightness or darkness purely based on imagination. This is the art of suggestion; the art of depiction using gestures and expressions. It expresses beyond the darkness of night, the longings of a beloved lit up by the subtlest light of a crescent moon or the twinkling stars in a black sky caught by the symbolic gestures formed by the deft fingers. The dancer can use a vast repertoire of movement to paint a detailed picture for the viewer, depicting all of these and more.

The dancer looks beyond her body at a landscape of fantasy. Although she moves in spaces which are defined by the formal performance stage or arena, her skill is tested when she breaks the barrier of mere formality and kindles the viewer's vision to see the entire Universe. As she performs, she becomes the Dance of Shiva and speaks to you of the cosmos. With her arms moving in space, her legs change postures in quick succession to keep up with the rhythm struck by her feet. The dancer depicts the starry sky, the thundering clouds, the light of dawn, the movement of the planets, the burning glow of fire and the sweeping turbulence of the wind. Nature is captured through the use of symbols, suggestions, rhythms and melodies. As the dancer transforms into the power behind the dance – the King of Dance – she simultaneously becomes the "*adimai*" – a slave of a force which is beyond her – the force of Nature and its ever-changing moods.

Drama is inherent in dance. Deep and sombre shades are created through movement and expressions. Radiant and awe-inspiring images are crafted on the stage to narrate profound ideas. A battlefield of gloom is depicted through specific gestures and a vast sweep of the arms. The pathos is reflected in the dancer's eyes. They are the eyes of Arjuna as he sees his kith and kin destroyed in battle in the epic, The Mahabharata. His despondency is like a barren desertscape. His eyes hold no hope. But soon he is made to "see" differently. Krishna

extols the Bhagavad Gita and brings to light the meaning of eternity.

This desolate scene springs to life like the *muktadhara* – the gush of water from the unseen heights of the waterfall. Darkness and light vie with each other – the shadows cast by Arjuna's doubts and misgivings are dispelled by the light and benevolence of Krishna's teachings. In a series of contrasting images, each created through varying degrees of light and shade, a narrative unfolds. It culminates in the enlightening luminosity of the "*Vishwa Roopa*" – the indescribable, infinite image of the Lord. It is formless like a cloudless sky and awe-inspiring like an unscaled snow-covered mountain peak. The dancer depicts this dramatically charged narrative with swift motion, breathtaking stillness and tender subtlety. Like a photographer, she captures the moment and colours it with her own imagination.

With a mere quiver of the lips, a glance, a smile or a twitch of the brow, the dancer creates a rainbow of emotions. *Shringara*, or Love, has many attendant images. The *Nayika* in love is afflicted by the beauty of Nature. Cool winds burn her with desire. The clouds are her messengers to her beloved. Love birds become her confidants. The waves of water she sees seem to be as turbulent as the pangs of her lonely heart. Flowers bloom everywhere, just so that her eyes turn away from the arrows of Cupid. The cool rays of moonlight hurt her for she is listless with longing. Her face is a landscape of love, longing, joy, despondency, anticipation, excitement, pleasure, pain, anger, doubt, jealousy, envy, sorrow, pity and finally, peace. The deep shadows, as well as the bright lights, of this moodscape are painted by the dancer's imagination and the poet's fancy. But finally, it is the eyes of the beholder that capture the image of *Shringara.*

A dancer can move away from the finely crafted details of emotion to abstraction by occupying a larger space in her movements. Torrential waterfalls, breathtaking sunsets, meandering valleys and awe-inspiring mountains become the architectural edifice created by her dance when she commands *Nrtta* and *Nritya* – the pure abstraction of movement and the expressional forays of dance – to speak with eloquence. Energy leaps out of the dancer's body. Like a gymnast conquering the limits of endurance, she unfolds a wide canvas that mirrors Nature. Dance, after all, imitates Nature. And therein lies the secret of Dance!

Lakhsmi Vishwanathan is a renowned exponent of Bharatanatyam. She is also a teacher, choreographer, scholar and author. Lakshmi is a master at the art of abhinaya or facial expression, filling the space with colour, mood and meaning. She is a recipient of the Presidential Award for Dance and senior research fellowships from the Ministry of Culture. She has authored several books – Bharatanatyam the Tamil Heritage, the best-seller Kunjamma, Ode to a Nightingale – a biography of M.S.Subbulakshmi and Kapaliswara Temple – the Sacred Site of Mylapore. Her next book Women of Pride, on Devadasis, is to be published soon. Lakshmi has danced, taught and lectured in fifteen countries around the world. She has performed at the famous Jacobs Pillow Dance Festival in the USA.

◄ Sarawak, Borneo

Hawkshead, England

Hawkshead, England

Sarawak, Borneo

Sariska, Rajasthan

Sarawak, Borneo ►

Sabah, Borneo

Sabah, Borneo

Agatti, Lakshadweep

Agatti, Lakshadweep

Taman Negara, Malaysia

Sabah, Borneo

Taman Negara, Malaysia

Ullapool, Scotland

Snowdonia, Wales

Rangdum, Ladakh

Sarawak, Borneo

Endau Rompin, Malaysia

Endau Rompin, Malaysia

Zanskar, Ladakh

Nameri, Assam

Taman Negara, Malaysia

Kuala Lumpur, Malaysia

Sariska, Rajasthan

Taman Negara, Malaysia

Endau Rompin, Malaysia

Sariska, Rajasthan

Dublin, Ireland

Sarawak, Borneo

Danum Valley, Borneo

◄ Endau Rompin, Malaysia

◄ Hawkshead, England

Taman Negara, Malaysia

Sarawak, Borneo

through my lens

mahesh nair

What is photography and what is a photograph? Wikipedia defines "photography" as *the process of recording pictures by means of capturing light on a light-sensitive medium.* Photograph is defined as *an image created by light falling on a light-sensitive surface, usually a photographic film or an electronic imager such as a CCD or a CMOS chip.* Wikipedia also traces the etymology of the word photography. Interestingly, photography comes from the French "*photographie*" which is based on the Greek words *phos* (light), and *graphis* (stylus, paintbrush) or *graphê* (representation by means of lines or drawing), together meaning "drawing with light." So, the essential element for photography, apart from the photographer, the subject and the camera, is light.

Though the principle of photography was thought to have been invented by Ibn al-Haytham (965–1040 AD) who invented the camera obscura and pinhole camera, photography as a practical process goes only as far back as the 1820s when chemical photography was developed. The first permanent photograph was an image produced in 1826 by the French inventor Nicéphore Niépce. At that stage, a picture took eight hours to expose and photography became viable only with the development of the daguerreotype by Louis Daguerre in 1839.

Although William Fox Talbot had invented the calotype process for creating negative images by 1840, it was finally John Herschel who invented the cyanotype process and also used the terms "photography", "negative" and "positive" for the first time. He discovered the sodium thiosulphate solution that could be used to "fix" pictures and make them permanent. In late 1839 he made the first glass negative. Many advances in photographic glass plates and printing were made through the 19th century and in 1884, George Eastman developed the technology of film to replace photographic plates, leading to the one used by film cameras even today.

In 1981, almost a century later, Sony unveiled the first consumer camera – the Sony Mavica – to use a charge-coupled device for imaging, eliminating the need for film. While the Mavica saved images to a disk, the camera was not fully digital and the images themselves were displayed on television. Nine years later Kodak unveiled the DCS 100, the first commercially available digital camera and the digital revolution in photography came into being.

While everyone agrees on the definition and the techniques of photography, the question that has been debated for years is whether a photograph is just a record of a given moment or does it transcend that specification and move into the realm of creativity and art. So, is photography an art form? Is the camera analogous to the brush of Van Gogh or is it just an instrument meant to be used for the mechanical reproduction of a moment in time? The debate occurs more so because of the so-called objectivity of the photographic medium as compared to any other visual art form.

The main purpose of photography has traditionally been to register reality and the debate regarding its genre has been

raging since the early twentieth century when photographers like Alfred Stieglitz, Edward Steichen, John Szarkowski and Edward Weston spent their lives advocating photography as a fine art. However, like in much of the art world, photography has also passed through several phases during its evolutionary journey.

At first, fine art photographers tried to imitate painting styles often using soft focus for a dreamy, "romantic" look. This movement, called "*Pictorialism*", gained enormous popularity through the works of such photographers as O. J. Rejlander and Henry Peach Robinson, who created sentimental scenes by printing from multiple negatives. Julia Margaret Cameron blurred her images to achieve a painter's softness of line, creating a series of remarkably powerful soft-focus portraits of her celebrated friends. In reaction to that, Weston, Ansel Adams and others formed the f/64 Group to advocate "*straight photography*", a form in which the photograph was a sharply focused reproduction and not an imitation of something else.

The debate still rages on. In addition, the advent of digital photography has changed the landscape completely. The before and after difference at a technological level is simple. Earlier, the photograph could either document reality or could move into the realm of art by using various techniques including aesthetic composition and the imaginative use of light. Today, with digital technology and superb software, the photograph can be manipulated in several ways, so that the end result has nothing to do with reality as perceived by the cameraman. In essence, even documentary photography could lose its objectivity since an event can easily be created on the computer through digital manipulation. This ability has completely changed the principles of photography over the past few years and will further evolve new styles in the future.

For argument's sake, if earlier, there were two streams of photography – documentary and artistic, the digital revolution will add a third stream which I would call "Digital Art Photography". This would help create a new form of visual art which, though rooted in the reality of a photograph, will lend the photographer the ability to freely express his artistic intent much like a modern-day painter. However, tor this, one would need to be skilled not only with the camera, but with the computer as well. Hence, the photograph will move from being a reflection of reality to a creation of one's imagination.

As is common for any new and emerging area, the opinions are firmly divided down the middle on whether or not this is acceptable. The purists from amongst the photographer community argue that this dilutes the skill of a photographer. But the reality is that this change is here to stay and several photographers embracing it as well. If current trends are to be believed, this form of art will gain further momentum in times to come. Any photographer who sees beyond the obvious and captures the essence of the moment transcends the role of a documenter and moves into the realm of

creative art. The role of photography as a medium of reality blends into photography as an art form and a medium of the imagination.

When I first tried my hand at photography, the notion of the photograph as a mechanical reproduction of a scene versus being a digital output of art fascinated me. My experimentation was aimed at determining if the photograph could transcend the reality reproduction without moving into purely computer manipulated images. To me, the fascination was in going beyond the obvious, to capture the essence, the unseen and the unsaid, so to speak. With nature as my subject, I found that I could easily use known techniques and play with natural light to create scenes that were very dramatic.

Light, or to be more precise, the play of light and the shadows that it creates fascinate me. As a child, it fired my imagination. I would live in a world of ghosts and make-believe creatures. At night, I watched the shadows that crossed my walls with fascination. When sunlight streamed in through the curtains of my windows and created new forms, I let my imagination fly. Now, from behind my lens, I am left engrossed by the beauty that it lends to nature. Light in its myriad avatars is all around us but usually we do not notice it. Over the centuries it has fascinated and captured the imagination of people from all streams of life. Even religion uses light to capture our most precious auras. Look around and there is light playing around us, over us.

My journey with nature started some time ago when I tried to capture its beauty through my lens. As I delved deeper into capturing that splendour, I realized that what makes the difference was just light... and its play. From simply capturing the beauty of nature, I found myself looking for compositions where light made Mother Nature even more fascinating – be it the majestic mountains with their snow-capped peaks, the vast undulating sea, the shadows in a verdant forest or the cracked and parched earth in the desert.

This book looks at light and the way it affects us. And it does affect us every day, every night, all the time – from the first cry of a new born baby to the time that our eyes close for the last time. *Let There Be Light...* is a tribute to this ultimate resource and my somewhat inadequate journey to capture those moments that show Mother Nature amidst light – suffused, diffused, enveloped, penetrated, enhanced - in the

After two successful decades in the corporate world, Mahesh Nair took to professional photography in 2005. His chosen area of work – nature and wild life – has taken him all over the world. His experience with various ecosystems turned him into a nature lover and conservationist since he firmly believes that without caring for our planet, there will be no more subjects left to shoot! Mahesh's works have been exhibited and auctioned several times in the short span of two years. Apart from photography, he also works with NGOs to promote awareness and need for nature and wild life conservation.

Agatti, Lakshadweep

Burren, Ireland

Burren, Ireland

Agatti, Lakshadweep

Danum Valley, Borneo

Danum Valley, Borneo

Pabitora, Assam

Dublin, Ireland

Glencoe, Scotland

Killarney, Ireland

Pabitora, Assam

Sarawak, Borneo

Acknowledgements:

The list of people who inspired, helped and encouraged me in my new career is very long. In fact, it is quite amazing how everybody encouraged me when I announced that I was switching careers at the age of 44! There are a few people, however, that I must mention here who went out of their way to help me on this path. Hopefully, as I try to live up to their expectations, this book is the first of many milestones. Rajeev, an exceptional architect and a friend, is the first to have pushed me into moving my body of work into the public domain rather than showcasing it only for my friends and family. Alka decided to curate my first solo exhibition as well as edit this book. Paresh, Paulo, Prof Pal, Naveen, Santosh, Prof Kapoor and Lakshmi, despite their busy schedules, met the deadlines and wrote articles that have enriched this book immensely. Sanjeev Saith helped me in photograph selection; my learning has been immense in the hours that he spent with me, during which time I picked his brains for his expertise. Parthiv and Shraboni put up with all my idiosyncrasies as they designed the book. Sonal patiently edited the articles and Pramod of Roli Books agreed to publish the book. All of them need a special mention here. Last, but definitely not the least, I wish to express my utmost gratitude to those who silently encouraged me on my journey. My parents, who, though shocked to hear my plans for a new career still stoically stood by me. My many friends who encouraged me and helped me tide over the many doubts and misgivings that I had. Balan, a superb photographer, my friend of many years, my guide and most vociferous critic. My long-suffering wife, Nilanjana and my son Nilesh who introduced me to nature and its beauty and weathered many "working holidays" and held my hand through the last few years. All these people were there beside me to cheer and blow away the myriad doubts that clouded my enthusiasm from time to time. To all of you a big Thank you!